G is for Granite

A New Hampshire Alphabet

Written by Marie Harris and Illustrated by Karen Holman

My thanks to my editor, Heather Hughes, Charter Weeks, the poets of Skimmilk Farm, NH State Architectural Historian James Garvin, UNH History Professor Jeffrey Bolster, Christa McAuliffe Planetarium Director Jeanne Gerulskis, John Barr, USMC Ret., Sebastian Matthews & his UNCA writing class, David Goodwin, Lynda Brushett, and Barrington kindergarten teachers Pam Lenzi and Deborah Delatore. Each of you has helped me make this a better book!

—*Marie Harris*

I would like to thank Marie Harris and Heather Hughes for giving me this wonderful opportunity. I thank all my family and friends for their unending encouragement and support.

And a special thanks to my Mom and Dad who taught me to believe that all dreams are possible.

—*Karen Holman*

Quotation within the illustration "S" is from the poem "July" © 1984 by Elizabeth Knies (FROM THE WINDOW; Teal Press). Used with permission.

Sleeping Bear Press
310 North Main Street
P.O. Box 20
Chelsea, MI 48118
www.sleepingbearpress.com
1-800-487-2323

Printed and bound in Canada.

Library of Congress Cataloging-in-Publication Data
Harris, Marie.
G is for granite : a New Hampshire alphabet / written by Marie Harris ; illustrated by Karen Busch Holman.
p. cm.
Summary: Illustrations and rhyming text, along with more detailed information, present facts about the history, culture, and landscape of New Hampshire.
ISBN 1-58536-083-X
1. New Hampshire-Juvenile literature. 2. English language-Alphabet-Juvenile literature. [1. New Hampshire. 2. Alphabet.] I. Busch Holman, Karen, 1960- ill. II. Title.
F34.3 .H37 2003
974.2—dc21
2002014405

On May 5, 1961, Alan B. Shepard Jr.— from the town of East Derry—became the first American in space. His space capsule was called the *Freedom 7*. Ten years later, he flew to the moon on *Apollo 14*. One of the things he did when he walked on the moon was to hit golf balls with a homemade club!

Christa McAuliffe was a high school teacher in Concord when she was chosen to be our country's first citizen-astronaut. She planned to teach two lessons while she was on board the space shuttle *Challenger*. But on January 28, 1986, just 73 seconds after lift-off, the shuttle exploded and all seven astronauts died. The whole country mourned. Today, however, programs at the Christa McAuliffe Planetarium and the Alan B. Shepard Discovery Center keep her message alive: "I touch the future, I teach."

New Hampshire can be proud of other astronauts with ties to our state including Commander Richard Searfoss and Mission Specialists Dr. Richard Linnehan and Dr. Lee Morin.

A is for Astronauts

Alan and Christa were space pioneers.
Looking toward Mars
and faraway stars,
they left the Earth to explore new frontiers.

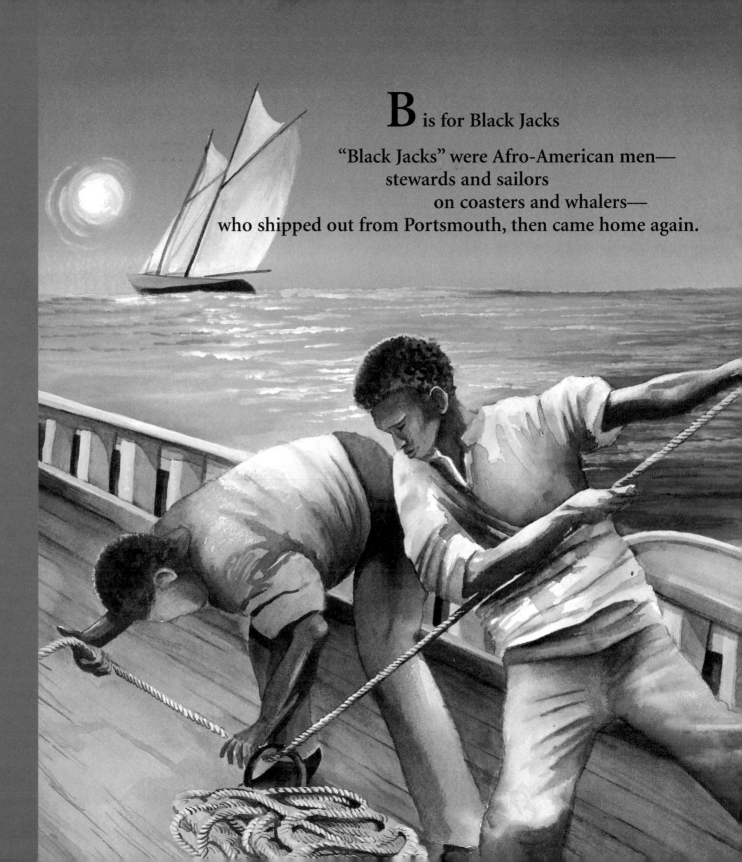

B b

B is for Black Jacks

"Black Jacks" were Afro-American men—
stewards and sailors
on coasters and whalers—
who shipped out from Portsmouth, then came home again.

In the 18th century, sailors were called "Jack Tars." African-American sailors were called "Black Jacks." They worked on ships as able-bodied seamen as well as cabin boys and drummers. They were brave men who faced great dangers at sea. And they were always at risk of being captured and sold into slavery.

Portsmouth has been home to the greatest proportion of the state's African-American citizens. The city has a Black Heritage Trail that tells many of their stories.

Augustus Saint-Gaudens—a sculptor whose studio was in Cornish—created the Shaw Memorial, a portrait of the first African-American regiment raised in the North to fight the Civil War. It can be seen on the Boston Common.

CONCORD
COACH

DEPARTS AT 2:00 P.M

Concord became our state capital in 1807.

For more than a hundred years, the Abbot-Downing Company was famous for making coaches built of the finest woods with flat tops for baggage and rounded bottoms resting on leather straps to make the ride comfortable. They were brightly painted and decorated. Inside, the seats were leather or various types of cloth, as the customer might prefer, and the metal hardware was polished to a shine. Concord Coaches traveled all over the country, pulled by big teams of horses. If you watch a movie about the Old West, you will probably see a Concord Coach.

The Abbot-Downing Company also made two-wheeled vehicles called the "one horse shay." They built carriages to take city people back and forth, and circus wagons, and wagons for bakers and grocers and chair makers. They even built streetcars with sled runners for snowy winter streets.

C is for the Concord Coach

From east coast to west coast the Concord Coach rolled,
through cities and fields,
"a cradle on wheels,"
carrying passengers, mailbags, and gold.

The white-tailed deer is New Hampshire's state animal. In the summer, its coat is reddish-brown; in the winter, grayish-brown. Its tracks look like hearts split in half. Deer prefer to graze for food at night. They eat green plants and all kinds of nuts. In the winter, they nibble on the twigs and buds of trees.

The purple finch is our state bird. The white birch is our state tree. The brook trout is our state's fresh-water fish.

D is for Deer

White-tailed deer graze under maples and birches—
does and their soft fawns,
bucks with their sharp horns—
all through the woods where the purple finch perches.

E is for Eagles

Here where clear waters reflect the clean air,
look to the deep sky,
up where big birds fly.
See! Against white clouds...a bald eagle pair!

Once there were many eagles in our state, especially along the banks of the big rivers and lakes, and around Great Bay. They found plenty of food, and they made nests and raised their young undisturbed. As people began to build houses and roads, the eagles were pushed out. By 1949 there was not one left at all! It was not until the 1980s that the eagles started to return. They are now a "protected species," so perhaps soon there will be as many eagles here as there were in the old days.

There's another special eagle in New Hampshire. It was carved out of wood a long time ago, covered with a thin film of pure gold called "gold leaf," and put on the top of the State House dome. Its head faced left—the direction of the "war eagle." After more than one hundred years out in the weather, it was taken down and put in a museum. A new eagle, made of strong copper and also covered with gold leaf, is now on our State House. This eagle's head is facing right, the symbol of a "peace eagle."

Robert Frost is one of the most famous poets in the world. He was born in California and lived in Massachusetts, New Hampshire, and Vermont. He even spent three years in England where his first two books of poetry were published.

In the beginning, Frost was a farmer by day and a writer by night. He wrote some of his early poems at the kitchen table in his farm in Derry, New Hampshire, working long into the night as his wife and children slept. Later, he lived for a while in Franconia, a small town in the White Mountains. His poetry became widely read and highly praised. He was a very popular teacher at schools, colleges, and universities. Frost won many awards and he recited his work at the inauguration of President John F. Kennedy in 1961. He lived to be almost 90 years old.

A good way to get to know Robert Frost is to read his poems aloud. One of his best-known poems is *Stopping by Woods on a Snowy Evening.*

F is for Robert Frost

Frost is a poet of countryside things:
    stone walls and hay rakes,
      stoneboats and snowflakes,
    orchards and woods where the ovenbird sings.

In the early days, before there were good roads, farmers and other settlers looked for a sure way to get their goods to market. The river was the best choice, but they needed a rugged boat to carry heavy cargoes—such as mast logs, stone, hay, coal, and all kinds of farm produce—up and down the powerful Piscataqua River between Portsmouth and the towns around Great Bay.

They designed a barge with an enormous canvas sail—called a lateen rig—that captured enough wind to power the boat they called a gundalow. The sail could be lowered to let the barge pass under the river's many bridges, then quickly raised again to keep going.

In 1982, an exact copy of a traditional gundalow, named for the last gundalow skipper, was launched in Portsmouth. You can climb aboard the *Captain Edward H. Adams* and imagine you're a deckhand!

G is for Gundalow

This rugged sailing barge, steady and slow,
hauled without number
bricks, apples, lumber
down from the farms to the city below.

Sarah Josepha Hale wrote a successful novel and composed many poems, including the famous "Mary Had a Little Lamb." She was the editor of *Godey's Lady's Book*, the first magazine of its kind in the country. Sarah Hale promoted the education of women, and she worked hard to see that Thanksgiving would be proclaimed a national holiday to celebrate the American home as a place of gratitude, joy, and sharing.

Many important women are associated with New Hampshire: Pioneer Molly Stark, Christian Science founder Mary Baker Eddy, composer Amy Beach, painter Elizabeth Gardner Bouguereau, Shaker Eldress Bertha Lindsay, novelists Grace Metalious and Louise Erdrich, photographer Lotte Jacobi, skier Penny Pitou, golfer Jane Blalock, poets Maxine Kumin and Jane Kenyon, movement theatre artist Marguerite Mathews, historian Laurel Thatcher Ulrich, and so many more!

H h

H is for Sarah Josepha Hale

Sarah Hale wanted a Thanksgiving Day
when families would gather
for feasting and laughter,
celebrating the American way.

I is for Isles of Shoals

Pirates, explorers, deep-sea fishermen,
poets and artists,
summertime tourists...
listen for foghorns and tales on the wind.

Nine small, rocky islands poke out of the sea about ten miles from Portsmouth Harbor. In 1614, Captain John Smith mapped them. Fishing families lived there. Sailing ships were wrecked there in dreadful storms. It is said that Blackbeard the Pirate buried a treasure somewhere on the islands. Some say that ghosts still walk these isles!

At one time there were grand hotels on the islands and tourists came from far away to stay for weeks in the summer. A famous poet named Celia Thaxter lived on Appledore Island; her father was the lighthouse keeper. Celia wrote poems about the isles and she had a beautiful garden. Many artists and writers visited to paint landscapes and talk about poetry. Today we can visit the Shoals by ferry boat and see Celia's cottage and garden.

Celia had a friend who was also a writer. Thomas Bailey Aldrich lived in Portsmouth and was the author of a popular novel called *The Story of a Bad Boy*. Some other writers who have lived and worked in New Hampshire are Ogden Nash, Thomas Williams, Wesley McNair, Donald Hall, Russell Banks, and Charles Simic.

Ii

The Abenaki people lived all over the northeast part of the United States and Canada. They built their villages along rivers. Their houses—called wigwams—were made of sapling frames covered with bark shingles. They used canoes to travel and they carried smaller wigwams when they were away from home. Abenakis were farmers, hunters, and fishers. Some Abenaki still practice the craft of basketmaking using ash wood and sweet grass. But there are few people still alive who know the old ways.

Chief Joseph Laurent was one of the first to write down his people's language. His son, Stephen Laurent, spent more than 30 years translating the first dictionary of the Abenaki language. In 1988, his words helped save his father's store in Intervale. It is now a national historic site.

Lake Winnipesaukee is the largest of New Hampshire's 2,000 lakes and ponds. The Abenaki word Winnipesaukee means region of the lakes.

J is for Chief Joseph

Joseph Laurent was the first we have heard
to write in a book
the words that it took
to read Abenaki in English words.

K is for Kancamagus

There is a highway that winds through our hills:
named for "The Fearless One,"
he was a loyal son.
Tales of his bravery echo here still.

An Abenaki chief is called a sagamore. We remember the name of Passaconaway, a sagamore who kept peace with the early settlers. Legend says that when he died, he was carried to the top of Mount Washington on a sled drawn by wolves and then taken up into the sky. His son, Wonalancet, was a peacemaker, too. Wonalancet's nephew Kancamagus, The Fearless One, led a raid on Dover in 1689 to settle a score with Major Waldron who had betrayed Wonalancet's people.

L is for Lady's Slipper

Wild on the forest floor, palest of reds,
under the oak trees,
poking from brown leaves...
small satin slippers like under your beds.

The other name for this shoe-shaped state flower is "pink moccasin flower." It is one of the earliest woodland flowers of spring. Sometimes you can find hundreds of lady's slippers in one patch, but you should not pick them because they are fragile and might not grow back.

New Hampshire's state amphibian, the spotted newt, lives in ponds. In its immature form, the red eft, it is a bright red salamander that lives under the leaves on the forest floor.

In the old days, men, women, and even children worked in factories 11 hours a day, 6 days a week. The work was hard and dangerous. The biggest textile mills were owned by the Amoskeag Company in Manchester. In Berlin there were paper mills. Newport had woolen mills. There were shoe factories in Weare, Rochester, and other towns. The Belknap Mill in Laconia is the oldest brick textile mill in the U.S.

By 1901, it was the law that children had to go to school. There were other laws to say how many hours children could work and how old they had to be.

Many French-Canadian families worked in the mills. Their heritage is still felt everywhere in our state, from their roles in state government to their cuisine and traditional songs and dances and stories. Franco-American parties are called *soirées de rire*. The music that accompanies these "evenings of laughter" is often played on traditional hand-crafted fiddles.

m
M

M is for Mill Towns

Life wasn't easy in mill towns back then.
Grownups and children
woke up before dawn,
worked in the factories for hours on end.

In 1756, Daniel Fowle printed New Hampshire's first newspaper. Even now, besides the many other newspapers we have in our state, we can still read the *New Hampshire Gazette*, edited by Steven Fowle, a relative of Daniel Fowle, the paper's founder.

Another famous newspaperman from New Hampshire was Horace Greeley. He founded the *New York Tribune*, which stressed the need to end slavery in America.

N
n

N is for Newspaper

The oldest newspaper in all of the land:
the *New Hampshire Gazette*
is published here yet.
Pick it up free on a local newsstand!

O is for the Old Man of the Mountain

His unchanging profile juts through the clouds.
Through winter and spring rains,
and fall when the leaves change,
he watches the seasons beneath granite brows.

This "Great Stone Face" is New Hampshire's symbol. You can see him on coins and road signs and license plates and other places. His lined face is made of granite ledges. Granite is our state stone and New Hampshire is called "The Granite State."

The native people had known about this face on the mountain for a long time. He was "re-discovered" in 1805 by a group of surveyors who saw him reflected in the lake—now called Profile Lake—below him. Millions of people come from all over the world to see him and take his picture.

Once, the Old Man was so beaten by rain and wind and ice, he almost broke. Everyone worried that his "forehead" was about to slip off and break his "nose." In 1916 Reverend Guy Roberts found E.H. Geddes, a man who knew how to fix the face. It was difficult and dangerous work, but he did it! Since then volunteers have kept up the work, and today the Nielson family is in charge of inspection and repairs.

P is for Presidential Primary

Each of us votes for our own candidate.
Ours are the voices
that make the first choices.
That's why New Hampshire's "The Primary State."

Since 1920, New Hampshire has been the first state in the union to hold its presidential primary. Any natural born citizen of the United States, who has been a resident for 14 years, and who is at least 35 years old, and is a registered Republican or Democrat or Independent can file to be a candidate and run for president of the United States.

Also in 1920, Congress passed the 19th Amendment giving women the right to vote. A Dover woman named Marilla Ricker spent 50 years fighting for women's voting rights. Just two months before she died at the age of 80, the new amendment allowed Marilla Ricker to vote. Today, women serve in all areas of state government, from the office of governor to the legislature. Jeanne Shaheen was New Hampshire's first woman governor.

P p

Q q

Q is for Quill Pen

Quill pens are feathers for dipping in ink.
Back in the old days
they were the best ways
for writing down words to say what you think.

A quill pen is made from the flight feather of a goose, swan, peacock, or other large bird.

Many New Hampshire people used quill pens to sign important documents. William Whipple, Josiah Bartlett, and Matthew Thornton signed the Declaration of Independence. John Langdon and Nicholas Gilman signed the United States Constitution.

On October 12, 1853, at a meeting in Blake's Tavern in Exeter, Amos Tuck is said to have established the Republican Party. He believed in the abolition of slavery and helped elect Abraham Lincoln as the first Republican president.

Three New Hampshire men have served as U.S. Supreme Court Justices: Salmon Portland Chase, Harlan Fiske Stone, and David Souter.

R r

R is for Republican

Amos Tuck made a political plan.
He sharpened a quill pen,
signed what he'd written,
and so the Republican Party began.

Europeans were some of the first settlers in New Hampshire. Captain Walter Neal and his passengers liked this pleasant spot a few miles upriver from the sea and here they built a Great House. The little settlement on the banks of the river soon grew into a busy town. Strawbery Banke was re-named Portsmouth.

Today, in the old "Puddle Dock" neighborhood, some of Portsmouth's historic houses and businesses have been preserved as a museum called Strawbery Banke. (It still keeps the old-fashioned spelling.) You can walk the lanes of this "town-within-a-town" and catch glimpses of how people lived and worked from the 1600s to the 1950s.

July blows through the trees,

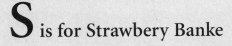

S is for Strawbery Banke

Up the Piscataqua, just to the west,
strawberries grew
and sailors then knew
right where a settlement would fit the best.

right through the center of town,
leaving a wide swath
redolent of roses and berries.
Elizabeth Knies

Tuckerman's Ravine is a huge, bowl-shaped basin on Mount Washington that was scooped out by the glaciers thousands of years ago. Every spring, long after the snow has melted from other slopes, people hike to the top of its high walls and ski—very fast!—to the bottom.

In 1642, Darby Field was the first white man to climb the mountain, guided by two Native Americans. In 1784, Jeremy Belknap, New Hampshire's first historian, accompanied a scientific expedition to Mount Washington.

In 1869, the first cog railway in the entire world steamed up the 2½ miles to the top of Mount Washington.

At 6,288 feet, Mount Washington is the highest peak in New England and endures some of the worst weather in the country. The strongest wind ever measured hit on April 12, 1934. It was 231 miles per hour!

T t

T is for Tuckerman's Ravine

Climb up to Tuckerman's, here's what you'll see:
  Snowfall the deepest!
    Ledges the steepest!
Only the daredevils come here to ski.

Samuel Wilson spent his boyhood and early manhood in New Hampshire. His nickname was "Uncle Sam." He supplied the Army with pork and beef in the War of 1812. He shipped the meat in barrels marked "U.S." for "United States." His workers joked that those initials stood for "Uncle Sam," and pretty soon people were calling the U.S. government "Uncle Sam."

U is for Uncle Sam

Sam Wilson's old house still stands in Mason.
He had a nickname
that brought him great fame:
"Uncle Sam" stood for the name of our nation!

U u

V

A village green is a large grassy area in the center of town, often shaded by trees, around which homes, stores, and large public buildings are clustered. Many small towns have an old-fashioned country store where they sell pickles from a barrel, maple syrup in jars, gingersnaps, and penny candy.

The town hall is where people get dog licenses and car licenses and other official papers. It's also the place where many towns hold Town Meetings so people can express their opinions and vote.

The first free, publicly supported library in the country was established in the town of Peterborough in 1833.

V is for Village Green

This is our village green...walk all about:
country store, town hall,
library, stone wall,
post office, firehouse...school's letting out!

W is for Daniel Webster

This is the lesson that Webster can teach:
when you have something
to say, and it's something
important, stand up! Make a speech!

Daniel Webster was famous for making speeches—called "orations." Born in Salisbury, he was a lawyer in Portsmouth before he moved to Boston. From there he went to Washington to serve in the House of Representatives, then in the Senate. Webster was the Secretary of State for three presidents: Harrison, Tyler, and Fillmore.

W
W

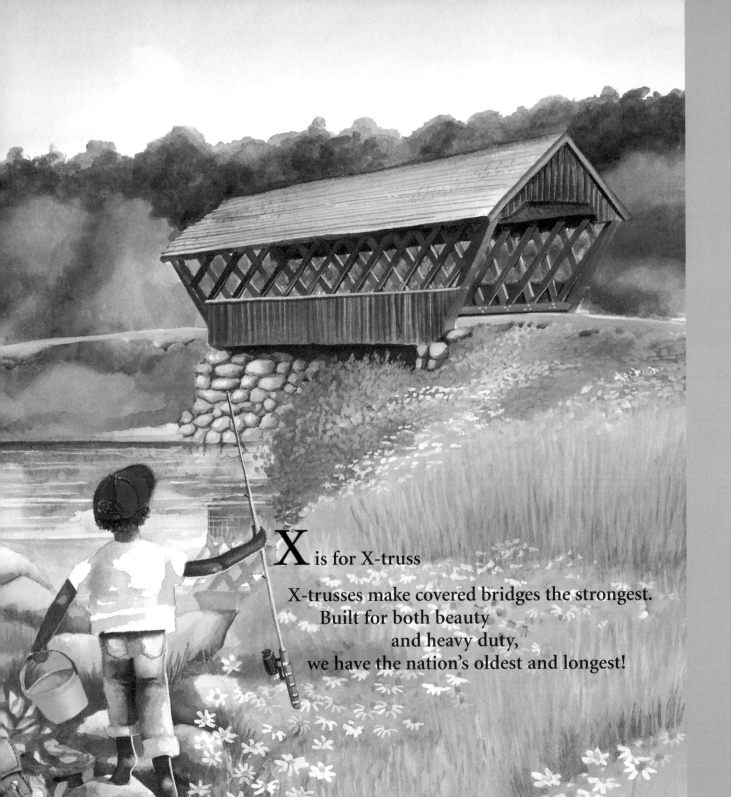

The covered bridge made crossing a river much easier and safer than riding a ferry. In winter, people used to shovel snow onto the bridges so the horse-drawn sleighs could pass easily across.

The braces for these bridges are called trusses. Can you see the **X**s? In 1830, Stephen Long of Hopkinton invented a truss that was more scientifically designed than others of the early 1800s. It was called the Long truss.

The bridge that crosses the Connecticut River between Cornish, New Hampshire and Windsor, Vermont is the longest one in the whole country! It is 449 feet and 5 inches long.

The bridge that crosses the Ammonoosuc River between Bath and Haverhill is our oldest one. It was built in 1829. The bridge was bypassed by a new highway span in 2000 and is now a pedestrian crossing.

X is for X-truss

X-trusses make covered bridges the strongest.
Built for both beauty
and heavy duty,
we have the nation's oldest and longest!

Franklin Pierce, known as "Young Hickory of the Granite Hills," was president from 1853 to 1857. One of the most important events of his term was the opening of Japan to world trade.

He was the son of a Revolutionary War soldier. He went to law school, then fought in the Mexican War where he was wounded. He served in the New Hampshire Legislature, the U.S. House of Representatives, and the U.S. Senate.

Pierce was the first president to have a Christmas tree in the White House. He also installed its first central-heating system and its first bathroom with hot and cold running water.

Another New Hampshire man—Henry Wilson—was President Ulysses S. Grant's second vice president in 1873. New Hampshire-born sculptor Daniel Chester French made a statue of Wilson's head and shoulders (called a "bust").

Yy

Y is for "Young Hickory of the Granite Hills"

Franklin Pierce was our fourteenth president.
First lawyer, then soldier,
and when he was older,
this handsome young man to Washington went.

Fifty thousand years ago, the Wisconsin Glacier came here and stayed for a long time. That was called The Ice Age. When it retreated, it left our state with beautiful deep valleys, tall waterfalls, winding rivers, and long lakes.

It can get really cold in New Hampshire in the winter. In fact, the coldest it's gotten so far was -46 degrees in Pittsburgh on January 28, 1925.

And there was the "Year without Summer" in 1816, when there was frost every month of the year!

In the old days, people "farmed" ice… they cut blocks from frozen ponds with big saws, stored them in sawdust, and sold them in the spring for refrigeration.

People in New Hampshire still go ice fishing on lakes and ponds. And we like to ice boat and ice skate, too!

Members of the University of New Hampshire's Women's Ice Hockey Team were part of the U.S. team that won an Olympic Gold Medal in 1998 in Nagano, Japan.

Zz

Z is for Zero Degrees (and below!)

Zero is just the beginning of cold.
Winter nights deepen.
Freezing winds creep in.
Plump up the comforters! Fill the woodstove!

A Stagecoach of Facts

1. What could be called the most unusual golf course in the universe?

2. Where can we see the work of Augustus Saint-Gaudens?

3. What vehicle was called "a cradle on wheels?"

4. What is our state bird and what state tree does it perch on?

5. What does "endangered species" mean?

6. What is a "lateen rig?"

7. Who wrote "Mary Had a Little Lamb?"

8. Where could there be buried pirate's treasure?

9. Who was a "sagamore?"

10. What is another word for a flower shaped like a shoe?

11. What was the largest mill in the world?

12. What is a "*soirée de rire*?"

13. Who was Horace Greeley?

14. What is one of New Hampshire's nicknames?

15. What is a "primary?"

16. What New Hampshire men signed the Declaration of Independence? The United States Constitution?

17. What was Portsmouth's original name and how would people spell those words now?

18. What is a "cog railway?"

19. Who is America's most famous "uncle?"

20. Where was the home of the first free library in the country?

21. What is an "oration?"

22. Why did people shovel snow onto a bridge instead of shoveling it off?

Answers

1. Astronaut Alan Shepard temporarily turned the surface of the moon into his own driving range in 1971.
2. The Saint-Gaudens National Historic Site in Cornish is open to visitors who can tour his studios and see many of the sculptures, reliefs, and medals he made.
3. Because of a unique suspension system, using leather "thoroughbraces," Concord Coaches were more comfortable than carriages that used springs. Mark Twain called the coach "a cradle on wheels."
4. The purple finch can often be seen in the branches of the white birch.
5. An endangered species is a group of living things—plants or animals—which are in danger of becoming extinct if their habitat is not protected.
6. That is the name of a particular kind of mast and sail such as that used on the gundalows. The design makes it easy to lower and raise the sail as the boat passes under bridges. It can be worked by one person alone.
7. Sarah Josepha Hale.
8. Legend has it that Blackbeard the Pirate buried treasure somewhere on the Isles of Shoals. Some say it's Appledore, some say Star or Smuttynose or it even could lie beneath the ground on tiny Lunging Island. And did Blackbeard really leave his 13th wife behind to guard his treasure?
9. A sagamore was an Abenaki leader or wise man. He was honored for his bravery as a hunter and warrior, his power as an orator, and his reputation as an honest and generous man.
10. The pink moccasin flower is another word for our state's wildflower, the lady's slipper. Real moccasins were made of animal skins by the Abenakis.
11. The Amoskeag Manufacturing Company, located on the Merrimack River in Manchester, produced textiles. By the turn of the 20th century, the mill complex was the largest in the world. It employed almost 17,000 people.
12. That's what Franco-Americans call an evening of songs and laughter. It's a party with friends and relatives.
13. Horace Greeley, born in Amherst, was the founder of the *New York Tribune*. He is often quoted as saying "Go West, young man!"
14. New Hampshire is called The Granite State because our mountains and hills are made mostly of granite. The state motto is "Live Free or Die," first said by General John Stark, a Revolutionary War hero.
15. In a primary election, people vote for the people they want to run for president of the United States. New Hampshire has held primary elections since 1913. The New Hampshire's primary is the first in the nation.
16. On July 4, 1776 William Whipple, Josiah Bartlett, and Matthew Thornton signed the Declaration of Independence for New Hampshire. On June 21, 1788, New Hampshire became the ninth state to approve the US Constitution and John Langdon and Nicholas Gilman signed it.
17. Strawbery Banke was what the first settlers called their new town. Today, "-bery" would have another "r" and "Banke" would have no "e."
18. In 1869, a railroad train ascended the 2.5 miles to the top of Mt. Washington. Designed by Sylvester Marsh of Campton, it was the first of its kind in the world. It is still in operation today. It runs on a track. The engine turns a "cog gear" and the whole train climbs tooth by tooth. The round trip takes about 3 hours.
19. Around 1812, Uncle Sam became associated with the United States. Imaginary versions of his face have been drawn for cartoon and posters since then. He is most often pictured with a white goatee and a star-spangled suit.
20. Peterborough.
21. An oration is a long speech that is spoken aloud. The best orators, like Daniel Webster, are eloquent—that is, they speak well—and succeed in convincing people of their point of view.
22. Because sleighs crossed covered bridges in winter, it was necessary to shovel snow onto them so the runners would slide.

Reference List

Brindell Fradin, Dennis. 1992. *From Sea to Shining Sea: New Hampshire.* Danbury, CT: Children's Press, Grolier Publishing.

Museum of New Hampshire History. 2002. [Online] www.NHHistory.org/museum.html

New Hampshire Department of Resources & Economic Development. 2002. [Online] www.dred.state.nh.us

New Hampshire Historical Society. 2002. [Online] www.NHHistory.org

New Hampshire State Government. 2002. [Online] www.state.nh.us

NH.com. 2002. [Online] www.nh.com

New Hampshire: A Worldwide Travel Guide. 2002. [Online] www.newhampshire.worldweb.com

SeacoastNH. 2002. [Online] www.seacoastnh.com

Yager, Ronald and Grace. 2000. *The Granite State: New Hampshire, An Illustrated History.* Sun Valley, CA: American Historical Press.

Marie Harris

Marie Harris, New Hampshire Poet Laureate from 1999-2004, has been writing poems since she was 8 years old. Her work has been published in literary magazines and books, including *Weasel in the Turkey Pen* (Hanging Loose Press) and *Your Sun, Manny* (New Rivers Press). She has edited several poetry anthologies and writes travel articles that are often illustrated with photographs taken by her husband, Charter Weeks. Marie and Charter live in the woods in a house they built by hand. In the winter they keep warm with woodstoves, and in the summer they tend a vegetable garden, swim in their pond, and go sailing on the ocean in a boat named *SENSEI*.

Karen Holman

Karen Holman was born in Montreal, Canada, but soon after moved to the United States, living in New York, New Jersey, and finally settling in New Hampshire. Although painting since the age of 10, her career focused on founding an interior architectural firm with offices in New York City and New Jersey in the 1980s. Her passion for art was much stronger, however, and she "gave it all up" in 1990 to focus on a career in art through graphic design and commercial illustration. She has continued to share her love of art by teaching children and donating illustrations for various publications. She lives in Salisbury, New Hampshire with her family and recently received a watercolor commission to design the poster celebrating the 100-year anniversary of 4-H in the state.